Creative Team

Co-founders & Directors
Debbie and Phil Waldrep

Creative Director
Thomas Schwindling

Head of Publishing
Mackenzie Borden

Content Editor
Jared August

KNOWN
A Six-Week Study on
Cultivating Biblical Community

Copyright © 2024
By Maegan Waldrep Schwindling

Published in Decatur, Alabama by Women
of Joy. Women of Joy is a registered
trademark of Phil Waldrep Ministries.

ISBN 978-1-7323687-7-4

@womenofjoy

womenofjoy.org
1.800.374.1550

This Study Belongs To

_____

_____

Start Date

_____ / _____ / _____

KNOWN

A Six-Week Study on Cultivating Biblical Community

Maegan Waldrep Schwindling

Maegan Waldrep Schwindling

It has been an absolute privilege growing up alongside Women of Joy since my mom and dad founded it in 1993. I am incredibly blessed to have crossed paths with countless remarkable women from all corners of the country. One of my favorite aspects of our ministry is the opportunity to minister to pastors and their wives in New England. Many of these women have become more than acquaintances– they are a part of my community. My most sought-after days are those I get to spend in Vermont with friends.

Through Women of Joy, we have the honor of listening to the stories of women from diverse backgrounds and ages from various corners of the country. Whether they're a pastor's wife in New England or attendees at Women of Joy, a common thread emerges– many women feel disconnected from the church and each other. It's a harsh realization that, in our modern world, we are the most connected we've ever been *and* the most lonely.

My hope is that you have embarked on this study because you, too, long to cultivate biblical community. While this study can be pursued individually, our prayer is that you might engage with others along the way. It might be a single friend, a small group in your home, or a group at your church. It all starts with conversation.

The truth is, we are not designed to navigate life in isolation, though we often convince ourselves that the small device in our purse is sufficient for connection. I am just as guilty as anyone when it comes to the allure of my phone, and I'm grateful for the bridge it creates between me and friends, miles away. But we must acknowledge that this isn't how we are meant to have relationships.

As we delve into the study, I pray you remain hopeful for what God can do through you in your own church and community. It is imperative that we continue to build these relationships to ensure that those who come behind us will do the same.

Maegan Schwindling

Maegan Waldrep Schwindling

Table of Contents

Introduction

Known

As my husband and I sat around our dinner table a few years ago, our discussion shifted to our current friendships. It was easy to count them. We could only think of two who lived locally! One for each of us. To be honest, though, these friends were our neighbors. They were stuck living near us. We considered them friends, but I suppose we didn't really know how they felt about us.

Throughout this conversation, many questions came to mind: Why didn't we have more friends? Weren't we fun people? Didn't we have something to offer? Why did we have so many close friends in other states but so few in our own city? Why is it so hard to build relationships as an adult?

I'd love to tell you that we quickly snapped out of this and moved on. But that would have been far from the truth. We had recently moved back to my hometown and the transition was difficult. I just couldn't figure out why people I had known for years weren't calling to hang out or go to lunch?

The worst part of moving? We were visiting churches once again. UGH. Just thinking about it makes me want to cringe. I'd rather hear nails scraping a chalkboard than endure another "welcome" time where we're forced to admit we're visitors!

Perhaps you can relate to this season of our lives. My husband and I started to believe that we weren't worthy of having friends. We grew defensive and questioned if people liked us or not. We began to feel that they were the problem. Not us.

A few months later, we sat around our dinner table once again. This time we discussed intentionality in our friendships. I had been thinking and praying about what made our out-of-state friendships so special. We had left a community we loved, a community where we were authentically known and where we really knew others. Did we make a mistake?

As we forced ourselves to wrestle with these hard questions, we realized that neither of us wanted to be open; neither of us wanted to be found. We said we wanted community, but we weren't really willing to open ourselves up to it.

In hindsight, the only thing we wanted was company. Why? The old saying is true . . . "Misery loves company." We wanted people to come over and tell us how awesome we were. We wanted people to agree with us on how terrible our lives were and how everyone else was wrong. The more we talked that night the more we realized we feared being truly known.

Community cannot flourish with complacency.

The words "grow" and "complacent" should not be in the same sentence. Relationships that do not move toward Jesus will never become biblical communities.

I'm happy to report that since those difficult conversations over a decade ago, God has graciously answered our prayers. He has provided us a deep biblical community in our local church body. It isn't a large group, but our relationships with one another are real and authentic. Jesus himself modeled this approach of investing in a core group of close friends. We will come back to this point later in our study.

Why this study?

The Women of Joy tours have provided the opportunity for us to get to know many of you and listen to your hearts. We treasure these conversations!

A frequent refrain we hear each year is how many of you long for biblical community – to be connected with a group of believers who genuinely care about each other. A Christian conference provides a burst of excitement and energy, yet even here, with five to ten thousand women worshiping our Lord side-by-side and learning together, it is easy to feel alone and unknown. How can we build lasting biblical community in our daily lives?

If you've wondered this before, then this study is for you!

For me, it took years studying Scripture to understand that there are no shortcuts to meaningful relationships in life. I had to make a conscious decision to invest in the people around me. I realized the importance of face-to-face interactions with others. Although, I still cherish my friends who don't live in my community, I have grown to dearly appreciate those in my daily life.

For those of you seeking to find your place in biblical community, here's the great news: Scripture gives us a guide to true biblical community.

My hope is to share helpful and practical tips from Scripture that have transformed how I look at relationships. Over six weeks, this Bible study will guide you on what it looks like to be known, how we can build intentional community, and how we can form lasting and life-giving friendships with others.

Why "known"?

It's easy to make a friend, but oftentimes what we want looks more like a one-way street. We want others to tell us everything about themselves and take the focus off of us. We hide our true selves and don't want to be known.

But can I encourage you that you really do want to be known? After all, you picked up this Bible study and you're willing to dive into studying Scripture in community. The most important step is simply to begin!

Let's journey together through the gospels and some of Paul's letters to see what Scripture has to teach us. If you are starting this Bible study alone, I want to challenge you to invite others to join you. At the very least, plan to discuss the material with those around you.

First, let's take a moment to think through two key questions.

- What is motivating you to participate in a Bible study on community?
- What has hindered you from building biblical community in the past?

If you are meeting with a group, use this time to get to know each other and share your responses. I want to challenge you at this first meeting to find something in your own story that brings you together. There is something that you ALL have in common. I promise. It might not be deep, but I guarantee you will find a common theme in all of your stories. If you are studying alone, what do you have in common with your current friends?

Second, let's establish some ground rules. These might just be for you or for the entire group. You might settle on only two or three, but let me give you some examples:

Our group is based around trust. Without trust, we don't have a safe place to study Scripture. This is a place where we can be honest with our struggles.

We should always believe that everyone is trying their best. Why does this matter? Some weeks you may not have all of your study done. You may not want to show up. Yet with this rule, everyone is always welcome. Why? We know that you are trying because you're committed to the group. We will hold you accountable, but we also understand that we are all human!

We have the tendency to linger when we are together so it can be helpful if we set a specific timeframe to meet once a week.

Now your turn . . .

Take some time to establish your ground rules and determine how you plan to hold each other accountable. I assure you that being in community requires self-discipline. Yet the time that you devote to each other is well-worth it.

Week One

1

Foundational Truth

It is easier to live life alone than to live in community.

This statement isn't likely how you imagined a Bible study on community to begin, is it? You might have come here seeking an easy answer, but I want to tell you that the easiest way is not always best. We as humans complicate things because sin complicates everything.

The most meaningful communities are the ones we work the hardest to build.

They're worth it because God gave Jesus on our behalf so He could have a relationship with us (John 3:16). That relationship cost God His son.

Biblical communities consist of meaningful and deep relationships that point us toward Jesus. **Living your life alone is living contradictory to how God created you.** You were created for a relationship with Him AND other believers. In fact, you will not fulfill God's purpose for your life without living in community with other believers.

Perhaps you're already convinced that we were created for community. Maybe you want to skim this week's study and move on to the nuts and bolts of how to build community. To be honest, I'd probably think the same thing too! Yet I believe that this week's study covers foundational truths from which all relationships grow.

I want to challenge you this week to be reminded of essential Scriptural truths. Ask God to reveal new things about Himself through His Word.

Read 2 Timothy 3:16 aloud together in your group. Write it here:

_____

_____

_____

In 2 Timothy, Paul writes his final charge to his dear friend and protégé, Timothy. It is believed that Paul wrote this letter from his prison cell around AD 64–65. As we read these familiar words, I wonder if the church today has lost its awe of the uniqueness of Scripture. This verse indicates that Scripture was given to man by the work of God's Spirit; it is "God-breathed." The words of the biblical authors are the very words of God Himself.

Notice how Paul is clear about the purpose of Scripture. It is useful for teaching, rebuking, correcting, and training in righteousness. This is based on the very specific reality that Scripture is the inspired and infallible Word of God.

How does our society view the Bible?

_____

_____

_____

Read the following verses and note what they teach about Scripture:

Psalm 119:160 _____

_____

John 17:17 _____

_____

Proverbs 30:5 _____

_____

What theme is carried through these verses?

_____

_____

_____

This is our starting point. Everything we believe about God, His Word, and—for our purposes—what His Word teaches about community stems from this truth. God breathed every word of Scripture for us. He wants us to enjoy a relationship with Him. Scripture is our guide.

Finish your initial group time or time with yourself by reflecting on a time when the Scriptures first became real to you. It is okay if this is the first time that the Scriptures are becoming real to you. That is exciting! You're in a safe place to learn with us. It doesn't matter if it was yesterday or twenty years ago. What matters is that the Scriptures are becoming real to you today.

Record your thoughts here following your initial gathering with your group:

_____

_____

_____

Application:

Reflect on the beginning of your own spiritual walk. If the opportunity arises, share your story of coming to know Jesus with someone. Allow yourself to sit around a table with someone new whether it is at a church meal, while you are on your work break, or even at a new mom's group. The challenge for this week is to start having new conversations and to take your regular conversations to a deeper level. Hold yourself accountable by taking this small step this week.

Group Time Notes

Day 1: The Beginning

We established in our group time that it is easier to do life alone than it is to live in authentic community. Yet God desires us to thrive in community with Him and with other believers. We also established that God isn't asking us to do anything He didn't do Himself. As we begin, let's go back to the beginning.

Read Genesis 1:1. Who was there in the beginning? _____

God chose to create us in His likeness. What does Genesis 1:26–27 tell us about ourselves?

_____

_____

_____

In Genesis 2:7, we see man come to life. God breathes life into Adam from the dust of the ground, the dirt. The NIV translation reads, God "breathed into his nostrils the breath of life." Remember 2 Timothy 3:16? It states, "All Scripture is God-breathed." In Genesis 2:7, the text indicates that God used both the dirt of the ground and His breath to create a human being. God breathed the first humans into existence just as He breathed out His Word.

God created us, humans, as intelligent beings. Within my lifetime, technology has advanced so much that huge computers once created by IBM can be made very small! So small, in fact, that I can now scan my watch to purchase items at a store. I am flying in a metal tube twenty-eight thousand feet above the ground as I type this sentence. We could go on and on about the intelligence of mankind. Human beings are incredible! However, no human can breathe life into anyone. God is the one who chooses when we are born and when we breathe our first breath. He also chooses when we take our last breath on this earth.

Take a moment to breathe. You've probably been so busy lately that you haven't stopped to ponder the fact that you are breathing. The American Lung Association says we take approximately twenty thousand breaths a day. I don't know about you, but that makes me feel very productive!

What are you thankful for that you got to do today because you have breath in your lungs?

_____

_____

_____

Let's continue. What do we find in Genesis 2:18?

_____

_____

_____

Let's summarize what we've learned thus far:

- God existed.
- God created man.
- It was not good for man to be alone.
- God created a woman.

Read the following Scriptures and note what they teach us about community:

Ecclesiastes 4:9–12 _____

1 Corinthians 12:12–27 _____

Hebrews 10:24–25 _____

Proverbs 27:17 _____

A former pastor of mine, Jay Wolf, often said, "We need Jesus, and we need each other." I always thought it was so obvious when he said it, however, I find more and more that I need this simple reminder. Adam not only needed God; he also needed Eve.

What are some ways you can be grateful today that God has welcomed us into His story?

_____

_____

_____

Scripture clearly teaches that jealousy is a sin. Let me be the first to point out my sin here. I have often been jealous of Adam and Eve in the Garden. Can you imagine their life? Genesis 3:8 tells us that God was present in the garden. Adam and Eve didn't have to go out of their way to meet with Him. He was already there in the garden, dwelling with them. Our minds cannot comprehend what this would have been like, yet it is an amazing picture to consider! Life wasn't complicated. As I write this, I have many open tabs and multiple complex thoughts running in my brain. For Adam and Eve, it was simple. It was just them and God.

God could and did dwell with His creation. That is how He designed it and how He desires it.

You can probably guess where we are headed next . . .

Read Genesis 3:6. What do we see happen here?

_____

_____

It was Adam and Eve's fault. Eve ate first and then offered the fruit to Adam. Adam and Eve chose to eat the forbidden fruit that God commanded them not to eat. Sin entered the world and immediately everything changed.

Have you ever sinned and then it seemed as if everything changed in an instant? You were gossiping about a friend to another friend and accidently hit send on the text to the person you were saying bad things about? Or you knowingly took your relationship with your male co-worker a step too far? The list could go on and on.

What is it for you? Write here an instance when either your sin or another's changed everything.

_____

_____

Suddenly, after Adam and Eve sinned, they realized their nakedness. Ladies, we all know it would be so much easier to not have to worry about clothes and to just be naked. This is probably not the most ideal sentence to write in a Bible study, but I'm just being honest. Can I blame Eve for my lack of ability to find something to wear? I know I could. But we know it is much deeper than that.

I love to put all the blame on Eve. I would be lying if I said I hadn't thought or said bad things about her. I act as though I would not have eaten the fruit. But the reality is, you and I have eaten *many* fruits that God has told us not to eat. I have, more times than not, chosen sin because I wanted it. It was more fun. It was more enticing. It was the easy way out.

Sometimes it is not just Eve we blame. It could be the person sitting in this Bible study right now that you tend to blame for sin in your life. You might blame a family member. Yes, we certainly have things that happen to us that are outside of our control. Those are not the things I'm talking about here. We can control our mouths and actions toward others. We make decisions to sin every day.

My mom and I recently attended a panel discussion on women in business. A young entrepreneur was asked what she believed to be the biggest relational issue facing women today. The room was waiting for a response, probably assuming it would be something involving men, but you could have heard a pin drop when she said that the biggest relational issue facing women today is other women. From where we were sitting, it was fascinating to see the looks on the faces of those around us. Why? We all recognized the truth in the statement: *the hardest people for women to get along with are oftentimes women.*

Why are we even surprised Eve took the fruit?

God created us to be strong kingdom builders, but we allow Satan to distract us as we tear down those with whom we should be in community.

Read 2 Corinthians 10:3–5. What does this passage tell us about our Christian walk?

The war is in our minds. *Every thought must be taken captive.*

What thoughts have you not taken captive today?

Eve immediately saw the cost of her sin. Again, in Genesis 3:8, what changed?

Relationships are typically the first things in our lives affected by our own sin. Sin impacts our relationship with God, which in return impacts our relationships with each other.

Is there a time in your life when sin impacted your relationship with God?

How did that sin impact your relationship with others?

Day 3: Redemption

I encourage you to take a deep dive into Genesis in a later small group study. Genesis continues with much human sin. We see a lot of grace from God. Although we often assume the Old Testament is not applicable or relevant for today, this is far from the case. The Old Testament is the foundation upon which our faith is built.

What is the sin you need to confess to the Lord in your life today?

_____

_____

As we move forward in Genesis, we see sin corrupted the earth. The people on earth became so corrupt that something interesting happens in Genesis 6:5–7.

What is God's reaction toward sin in these verses?

_____

_____

It is interesting to consider the word "regret," as in "The Lord regretted . . ." (6:6). This term indicates that God had a strong sense of sorrow. It does not mean that God changed His plan. He is omniscient; He is an all-knowing God. Is it often difficult to grasp all of this with our finite human minds? Absolutely.

Isaiah 55:8–9 tells us that God's ways are not our ways. We can have two responses to this information. We can try to take control of our situation, or we can rest in the arms of an all-knowing God.

It is of utmost importance for us to understand the depravity of our sin. It brings God much sorrow and it is not what He wants for us. As we move on from Genesis, we understand that God created us so we could have a relationship with Him. A vibrant community of believers can only come from a place of intimacy with God.

Let's fast forward.

We established earlier that God had a plan from the beginning. This plan involved the most important person in human history, Jesus.

Matthew 5:17 tells us that Jesus did not come to obliterate the law. He is the actual FULFILLMENT of the law.

Have you ever wondered why Jesus had to point this out to the Jews? The topics that Jesus taught felt radical to those who closely followed the law. He had to establish His purpose on earth.

Jesus redeemed humanity. It was one and done. His time on the cross, burial, and resurrection sealed the deal.

An example from the adoption community comes to mind. Our family has been woven together through adoption. I have often heard parents referring to their child as "being adopted." I know they mean well, yet the actual "adoption" was a one-time deal that took place in a court before a judge who gave the child your last name and made them part of your family. Your child is not continually being adopted over and over again. He or she is adopted.

Ladies, we can rest in the fact that Jesus truly paid it all on the cross. Every wrong we had done—all of our sin—was placed upon him. For us who have placed our faith in Jesus, we are not being redeemed. We are redeemed. Words matter so much in how we talk about ourselves before the Lord.

You were never meant to be good enough. You never even had to attempt to be good enough. ***Jesus is enough.*** Rest in this truth.

When did you first believe in Jesus?

Do you still have the wonder of your salvation?

Read the following verses: John 3:16, 2 Corinthians 5:21

What do these two verses tell us about our salvation?

We are the righteousness of God because of Jesus. Think on this truth as you go about your day today.

Day 4: What Next?

My sanctification journey started early in life. As I approach a new decade, I have now been walking with the Lord for longer than I had without Him.

I look back on many different seasons in life, both good and bad. I'll be honest that there have been times when I was far from the Lord. Yet the longer I have been a believer, the more I want to be with Jesus and spend time in His Word.

It is not normal to be a Christian and not want to spend time in God's Word.

You are likely a part of a small group and are studying this book because you want biblical community. Again, this only stems from a healthy relationship with God.

Sanctification is a theological term you may have heard at your church or in your personal study. I will add that when we use the word "theological" or "theology," we are simply referring to the concept of studying God. We could go into much more detail, but let's stick to this definition for our time together. Although you may not fully understand the details of how sanctification works, it is a vital part of our salvation. Sanctification is best described as our personal journey of becoming more like Christ during our time here on earth.

There is an order to our salvation (theologians refer to it as the ordo salutis). This process begins with God knowing that we would be in a relationship with Him, it includes our justification when we believe in Jesus, and it ends with our future glorification in eternity (Romans 8:28–30). Sanctification, or the process of being made holy, is in the middle. I'm in the middle. You are probably in the middle, too.

For many of us, "sanctification / the middle" is the longest part of our spiritual journey. It is not a straight line. You can look at many examples from the Bible and see how, similarly, our walk with Christ also includes high highs and low lows. However, in all of these situations we are moving toward the next step, which is our glorified state when we will be with Jesus.

The most beautiful part of our sanctification is that Jesus is with us. We get to abide with Him as we long to dwell with Him fully one day.

Read the following verses and note what they tell you about your sanctification journey:

Philippians 1:6 _____

1 Thessalonians 5:23–24 _____

Hebrews 13:20–21 _____

Draw a line of what you believe your sanctification journey has been like.

Here is what I believe mine is like . . .

My prayer for you over this six-week stretch is that you will fall more in love with the Scriptures. In so doing, my prayer is that you find biblical community.

Where are you in your sanctification journey? Are you seeking God daily? Is this your first Bible study? Take the space below and be honest with yourself. This is a critical step before you can be honest with others.

_____

_____

_____

_____

_____

_____

_____

_____

_____

_____

Day 5: Self-Reflection

Next week we will dive into learning about the early church. Yet I want us to address the word "church" now. Many of us, me included, would likely say that the church has hurt us. You may have been hurt by the church, betrayed by someone in the church, left out at church, or perhaps never attended church because of what you have heard others say about church.

Have you had a bad experience with the church? What was that like?

_____

_____

_____

Friend, I have to be honest with you. The church didn't hurt you. The church is made up of sinners. A human being, who is a sinner, within the church hurt you. I do not say this lightly. I could write a book on the topic from my own personal experience. I don't plan to do that, but you're not hearing from someone that has not experienced hurt within the church. I'm not minimizing any pain you may have experienced or my own. I'm just telling you that it might be time to seek healing or to try a different church. I have been saddened when friends tell me that they have walked away from church because of the sinful actions of humans.

The sin that happens within many of our church walls is a tragedy. It should make us sick. It should be dealt with swiftly and in a biblical manner.

That being said, the only person who should be on any pedestal in your life is Jesus. No one else deserves that seat and if you feel someone is there—you need to examine yourself and ask if they are an idol in your life.

Every person in any church leadership position will let you down. Any person in your life that has a pulse will let you down.

Here's the truth: the church is the Bride of Christ. It is the instrument by which we find and build a biblical community. At Women of Joy, our team often hears from women who desire to be speakers, be involved in large ministries, or grow a platform. My question to them is this: What is your involvement in your local church right now? More times than not, we either hear silence or how their church has hurt them and no longer works for them.

Women of Joy, other conferences, gatherings, and even community Bible studies do not replace the vital role of the local church.

God is not going to elevate you to a position to minister to women from multiple churches if you are not first serving within your own.

Read Matthew 16:18 and write it here:

_____

_____

The church as a whole is unwavering. It is far larger than any denomination and thriving all over the world. Why? *The church is God's and Satan cannot destroy it.*

We can rest in this hope. Christ watches over and protects His bride, the church. No human can mess it up.

Here are your reflection questions to finish the week as you prepare for your group time together. We will cover each of these questions every week as we walk this journey together toward building your biblical community.

What did God reveal about Himself to you in Scripture this week?

_____

_____

How did your understanding of a particular Bible passage deepen this week?

_____

_____

Are there areas of your life where you have struggled to trust God this week? What can you do to better surrender these areas to Him for next week?

_____

_____

How did you reflect God's Word toward others this week? Is there anything you need to confess to God or someone else?

_____

_____

Journal Your Journey

Prayer Requests

Week Two

The Early Church

Some of the times I cherish most with our friend group are our dinners together. I use the word "cherish" because you probably know how difficult it is to get busy people around a table together. It takes days of calendar planning, baby-sitters, and wellness. Sometimes we meet at restaurants, yet my favorite times have taken place in one of our homes.

Early on, we tried to be fancier than we are now. We'd grill or cook a big meal. The deeper our friendship grew, though, the less that mattered. We now often order take-out and gym clothes are welcome. It isn't about the fanfare. It's about the quality conversation that results from breaking bread together. It is the comfort of sitting across from someone who knows you, and being with people you can be honest with about life's circumstances.

Acts chapter 2 always catches my attention when it mentions that the early church "broke bread" together. My husband and I have found such value when people can gather together around food. I think this feeling is universal. Food breaks down barriers, slows us down, and opens doors to conversations. Fortune Magazine quoted Dr. Erin Michos as saying, "Sharing meals with others is a great way to reduce stress, boost self-esteem, and improve social connection."

I believe that sharing meals with others serves as an accelerator that builds meaningful community. It anchors memorable occasions in a shared experience. Perhaps you don't know where to start? Try inviting someone over for dinner. I guarantee you they'll be thankful, and you'll enjoy the conversation that results from it. Don't know what to cook? Order take-out. You can blame it on someone else if it tastes bad. Just try it! I'm confident you won't regret it.

The breaking of bread was a huge part of the connectivity between the members of the early church. This is something that hasn't changed over two thousand years.

I'd imagine the early church was not as rushed as we are today. They took the time to be with one another, to help, and know each other's needs.

Undoubtedly, much has changed over the years! Yet, Acts 2:42 tells us that the early church devoted themselves to the fellowship and the breaking of bread together. God created us with the need to be with each other as we saw from last week's study in Genesis.

We start our time together this week in the book of Acts. Here, you see the foundation of the early church. Who was part of this group? How did it start? What did they do? How did God bless it? We are going to dive into this and much more.

How does this fit within our need to be known and be in community?

It has everything to do with it! We established that our core relationship should be with Jesus and out of this, we ought to be in relationship with believers. The early church truly knew each other and grew together. God added to their number by the thousands. A significant reason for this was their commitment to community, to knowing and loving each other well.

First and foremost, what best describes you: (circle one)

Lots of friends   Core group of friends

No friends   Hiding from everyone

What worries you the most that people in this Bible study might find out about you?

_____

_____

_____

In what areas of life are you most lonely?

_____

_____

_____

What characteristics of the early church do you crave the most within your own community?

_____

_____

_____

_____

Are you hiding your gifts or was there a time you hid your gifts from others in your church because you were fearful?

_____

_____

_____

_____

Application:

This week, work on your personal prayer strategy for your community. We've seen that a foundation of prayer within Christian community moves God to answer in big ways. Consider the qualities you desire to build within your current relationships or in the relationships you seek. Examples of these qualities may include honesty, empathy, transparency, compassion, etc.

Group Time Notes

Day 1: The Starting Point

Have you ever found yourself in a situation where you felt completely unqualified? Perhaps you were just waiting for someone to let you know that you were in the wrong place, doing the wrong thing.

I remember the first time I drove a car alone. I sat there and felt shocked that I was actually trusted to operate a vehicle on the road! For you, it might have been when you moved into your first apartment. It could have been when you drove your baby home from the hospital for the first time. Or perhaps you felt your coworkers doubted that you knew how to do your job after you received your promotion.

The term often used to describe these types of scenarios is "imposter syndrome." We've all experienced this in some form or another. Forbes tells us that 75% of women in executive positions have experienced it in their careers. Imposter syndrome is often missed when talking about church; however, I'd venture to say it is the worst within the church. Why? Satan knows that imposter syndrome is a GREAT tool to keep you from using your gifts and serving others. You might be in Bible study right now wondering if people will figure out that you actually don't spend time with the Lord as often as you've led them to believe. First, we doubt ourselves. Then Satan fuels it to the point where we talk ourselves out of whatever we were planning to do.

The reality is that we rarely know what we're doing. ***Everyone is dependent on the Lord providing what we need to be successful in any given situation.***

What is a personal experience from your life when you faced imposter syndrome within the church?

_____

_____

_____

Read Acts 1:1–26.

The book of Acts opens with Jesus's ascension into heaven. In Acts 1:8, Jesus tells His disciples that the Holy Spirit will come to give power and then Jesus proclaims the great commission (see also Matthew 28:18–20). At this point, the Holy Spirit had not yet come. We read that everyone just stood there. I believe they were in shock that Jesus was leaving them. They knew He would, but now they actually had to do what He had called them to do.

We go on to read that the group returns to Jerusalem and lays the foundation for the early church. I can only imagine that they had imposter syndrome at this moment! They're told that they will be filled with an unknown power and perform miracles like Jesus. How could this be so? How could they continue the mission of their Lord?

What do we see was their reaction (1:14)?

Luke notes that the women, including Mary the mother of Jesus, were present with the group. What did they do? They prayed! I don't know about you, but when I feel inadequate, my first response is often not to pray. Our human response is often to equip ourselves with more knowledge and to fix the situation on our own.

Where are you on this line of prayer?

NOT OFTEN PRAYING   PRAYING WITHOUT CEASING

What is your first instinct when you want to solve a problem? What would change in your life if you started with prayer?

What are two things you believe God could do through your church—or even your own Bible study group—if you truly devoted yourself to prayer?

In Acts, we go on to see God work amidst their prayers. They appointed a new apostle after Judas had left them. Later, we see the Holy Spirit come on them at Pentecost.

All of these things were born out of prayer. Jesus leaves them . . . they return to Jerusalem and pray. Ultimately, the result of their prayer is the New Testament church we are a part of today!

Day 2: The Holy Spirit

Have you ever wondered what it was like to be on the other side of history? As believers—part of the church, the body of Christ—we do not know life apart from the Holy Spirit. There is so much for us to learn on this topic and there are many directions we could go from here. For a few minutes, let's consider some basics.

We know that our God is a triune God. What does this mean?

Read John 14:16.

What does this verse reveal about the Holy Spirit?

_____

_____

_____

This verse tells us that Jesus asked God the Father to grant us the Spirit of Truth. This explanation is helpful for our current focus. The Holy Spirit came at Pentecost (which we are about to see) and is the same Spirit granted to us at salvation.

We need the guidance of the Holy Spirit in our daily lives. *Jesus knew how hard this life would be and asked God to give us a helper.* (This can have different implications at times depending on where we are in our Christian walk.)

How does having the Holy Spirit at work within you influence your daily life?

_____

_____

_____

Read the following verses and note how they describe the Holy Spirit:

Matthew 28:19 _____

2 Corinthians 13:14 _____

Now read Acts 2:1–36.

When I read Scripture, I am amazed to read of the fulfillment of prophecy. Remember when we considered the importance of the Old Testament? The Old Testament provides the prophecies that we then see fulfilled in the New Testament. This provides assurance for us that the things we study in the Bible will come to pass in the future.

What four prophecies do we see fulfilled here in Acts 2?

1. _____
2. _____
3. _____
4. _____

Let me encourage you. Don't get overwhelmed! Perhaps the idea of the Holy Spirit is new to you. Or maybe you feel like you have a grasp on this part of the Trinity. Either way, this is why studying the Scriptures in community is valuable. We can learn more about our God through seeing how He works in each of our lives.

Take time to list thoughts and questions you have about the Holy Spirit here. You can even invite your pastor to come and share about the Holy Spirit during your Bible Study this coming week, depending on how comfortable your group feels discussing this topic.

_____

_____

_____

_____

_____

Day 3: The Church

We concluded last week by discussing how the church will forever endure and that humanity can't mess that up. The church is the Bride of Christ. Now as we continue in Acts 2, we read of the role of the church.

Start today by reading Acts 2:37–47.

We could spend a whole study just in this passage! My hope, though, is that we can consider some basics as to how the early church thrived and compare this with what we see today.

Have you ever noticed how one negative person can bring down the excitement of an entire room? Did you know that it takes ten to fifteen positive people in a room to overshadow that one negative person and his or her attitude? I am sure you can think of negative people in your life. Don't worry, you don't have to write them down.

Peter had a strong presence that we see in Acts 2. He brought together all the positive people. I would imagine that there were still negative people around (see Acts 2:13), but it didn't really matter. Why? God was at work.

What do we see in this passage?

People were convicted of sin. They repented and believed as Peter preached.

Henry Blackaby wrote a well-known Bible study entitled, *Experiencing God*. In it, he encourages his readers, "Find where God is moving and join Him." God was moving through Peter and the apostles here in Acts 2. People wanted to join God and experience what He was doing in their midst.

How is God moving in your church and in your life?

How do you share the hope of Jesus with others?

The early church was laser-focused on the gospel. This should serve as a reminder to us that the foundation of biblical community is the gospel.

No, you aren't going to be in constant conversation about Jesus with your friends, but the gospel is the foundation of our hope.

How often do you discuss your relationship with Jesus with those in your close community?

How can we be more intentional in asking open-ended questions of those we spend time with about their walk with Jesus? Be prepared to start adding this into your group time together if you're studying this with others.

Day 4: How to Be

Are you competitive? Recently, I led a group of young people through a community-wide challenge. We were the underdogs. We were not expected to win. It was a long eight-day challenge, yet in the end, our team won!

As we were going through this challenge, I had been writing this study on community. I had seen so many similarities between the early church and our competitive group of young people. In particular, three themes I saw throughout the eight days were their devotion, their *attentiveness*, and their *loyalty*.

This group *devoted* every free moment they had to this challenge. This brought about a level of *attentiveness* they had lacked in previous areas of life. Why? Because they REALLY wanted to win! They were focused on the goal. Lastly, they remained *loyal* to each other throughout the whole challenge.

Do you see where this is going? We've already read that the early church devoted themselves to prayer and the apostles' preaching. They also devoted themselves to each other. Luke paints the picture for us that they were a loving group of people.

Read Acts 4:32–35.

What does this passage show you about how the members of the early church interacted with each other?

_____

_____

_____

Check in with yourself: Are you still devoted to the church and to prayer? How is this demonstrated practically?

_____

_____

_____

Members of the early church were attentive to those around them. They wanted to further the gospel and that meant paying attention to what was happening around them.

What do you pay the most attention to around you? Be honest with yourself.

Do you find yourself more focused on what others can do for you rather than on how you can encourage others in their walk with the Lord?

What would our communities look like if we were solely focused on furthering the gospel, caring for each other, and looking out for those in need?

Day 5: Reflection

We will spend time next week considering the actual building of your community. We've laid a foundation thus far in our time together. The early church possessed vibrant relationships with Jesus. The Holy Spirit used them in miraculous ways.

I don't know if you're like me in this area of life. My career background is helping people solve their own problems. That is my definition of social work. We could use bigger words, but that is the gist of how I've spent my working years.

In my personal life, though, there have been seasons where I just wanted to point out where others were doing things wrong. I lacked the self-awareness to even solve my own relational problems. You already read in the introduction of this study about how for years, I was my own stumbling block when it came to building community and relationships.

I could have continued wallowing in self-pity. I instead learned to self-correct. I am grateful to the Lord for His grace in this matter.

Perhaps you could use an opportunity to reflect today, maybe even to self-correct. What have you noticed that you might need to work on after two weeks of this study? What can you tell your group or a friend that will help hold you accountable?

_____

_____

_____

_____

_____

_____

Next, I want to pause here and encourage you not to shame yourself. Today you can draw a line in the sand. Your past friendships may have been focused on the latest gossip or trendy fashion choices, but now you're ready to move forward with deeper friendships. You and your friends may still love shoes, travel, and other fun things, however, you're now ready for your friendships to be rooted and grounded in the gospel of Jesus Christ.

Here are our reflection questions to finish the week and for you to prepare yourself for group time. Again, we will cover these same questions each week as we walk this journey together toward building a biblical community.

What did God reveal about Himself to you in Scripture this week?

How did your understanding of a particular Bible passage deepen this week?

Are there areas of your life where you have struggled to trust God this week? What can you do to better surrender these areas to Him for next week?

How did you reflect God's Word toward others this week? Is there anything you need to confess to God or someone else?

Journal Your Journey

Prayer Requests

Week Three

3

Relational Models

Scripture is full of examples of various relationships. There are significant portions of the Bible devoted to teaching us about marital relationships (for example, Song of Solomon). There are specific friendships in Scripture that help us draft a blueprint for building biblical community. In Luke's gospel, he records various details that relate to friendships among women. These passages show us how Jesus cared for women and reveal the vital roles women have within the church body. This will be helpful for us as we journey toward building our own communities.

It is true that we don't need to learn about community only from women. Our close friend group consists of both men and women. Yet, we will spend this week continuing with Luke's words (he authored Acts) on women and their relationships with each other.

I would like to encourage you to start your group time by discussing why is it often so hard for women to be in friendship with each other?

Here are some limiting factors I would like for you to consider and discuss within your group:

1. Lack of trust - Henry Cloud says it best, "Trust is the fuel for all of life." Our lack of trust in others breeds an environment of loneliness. You have to trust in order to have a thriving community.

2. External pressure - There are popular sayings on social media discussing how we are to drink enough water, get our work done, act like we don't work, spend time with our kids, be there for our husbands, and not be tired. The external pressures that we face are real.

3. Comparison - I've talked to countless women who have missed out on amazing opportunities to find friendships because they continually compared themselves with others.

4. Competition - Life is not a race to see who is the most godly. It also isn't a competition to see who can seem the most put together. Life is hard. No one really has it all together, even if some claim they do.

I could write many pages on what limits our relationships. Yet, my hope is to consider these four factors in more depth as we consider examples of female relationships within the Bible.

Spend time discussing the following questions in your group or journaling if you are studying alone.

Who do you compare yourself to the most?

_____

_____

_____

What are some of the current external pressures in your life?

_____

_____

_____

Do you trust the people in your life? What causes a lack of trust?

_____

_____

_____

Who are you competing against? Is it a family member who gets more attention? Is it another woman within your church?

_____

_____

_____

Application:

We have considered limiting factors of relationships in our opener for this week. How can you be self-aware and notice when these factors influence your own life? How can you take every thought captive (2 Corinthians 10:5) to be good and fruitful?

Group Time Notes

Day 1: Naomi & Ruth

Perhaps you have studied the book of Ruth and the love story that unfolds between Ruth and Boaz. Today we are going to consider this biblical book from a different perspective, the perspective of a widow in need of help. Although Ruth is more than eager to help, her mother-in-law Naomi tries to avoid her assistance.

"I need help."

I doubt I am the only one who thinks these are three of the hardest words to speak. Naomi certainly wasn't going to ask Ruth for help!

Read Ruth 1:1–14

What happened to Naomi? Why is she mad at God?

_____

_____

Naomi was convinced she knew the plan for her life. This wasn't it.

In 1:13, Naomi proclaims that she is worse off than either Ruth or Orpah. Her lot in life is "exceedingly bitter." She believed there was still hope for Ruth and Orpah to find new husbands and to enjoy a prosperous life. But there was no hope for Noami. She knew she was too old. It would be near impossible for her to get remarried. In that ancient society, Naomi seemed destined for poverty and struggle. Life as she knew it was over.

Have you been faced with a situation when you believed life as you knew it was over?

_____

_____

Here's great news for us. *We don't get to decide when our life is over.*

You're reading this study. That means you have a pulse. *There is still work for you to do here on earth.*

I am so thankful we don't get to decide when God is done with us. He put us here for His glory.

Read Ruth 1:15–22

Does Naomi give up? Yes. Yet even as her faith falters, Ruth's commitment strengthens. Two of the most quoted verses in the entire book of Ruth are 1:16 and 17. Ruth's words here are beautiful, "Where you go I will go, and where you lodge I will lodge. Your people shall be my people, and your God my God" (1:16).

I have to admit, 1:18 is a personal favorite. Why? Samuel, the author of Ruth, provides the reader with a narrative summary of events. I essentially read Naomi as giving up and saying, "FINE."

Have you ever had a friend so adamant to help that you finally gave up and said, "FINE"?

Have you ever said "FINE" to God after you had been hesitant to trust His plan and walk in obedience?

The text states in 1:18 that Ruth was "determined." She was determined to leave all she had ever known in Moab. She was determined to travel with Naomi to her homeland of Bethlehem. She was determined to follow the God of Israel.

Does Bethlehem sound familiar? If you know the Christmas story, you might remember that Mary and Joseph also had to travel to the same town, Bethlehem.

At the end of Ruth, in 4:17, we read that Ruth and Boaz gave birth to a son, Obed. They eventually became the great grandparents to King David.

Why does this matter?

Read Matthew 1:1–17. In particular, focus on 1:5–6.

Today we know how the story ends. Many hundreds of years later, a descendent of Ruth is born in a stable and laid in a manger. His name is Jesus. Although Ruth and Naomi didn't know it at the time, we see how God used their situation as part of His plan.

What does this passage tell us about King David that is important in relation to Jesus?

_____

_____

_____

Ruth's trust and obedience made the way for Jesus to come to earth. It made the way for us to be with Him in heaven.

Naomi needed help. She didn't even want to receive help. Yet, our redemption was dependent on her trusting Ruth. In return, Ruth was obedient to God.

What does this mean to us?

- Naomi was convinced her life circumstances could not be redeemed. Yet God provided Ruth—a woman of faith and loyalty—to stand by Naomi's side. Furthermore, God provided Boaz—the son of a prostitute (Matt 1:5)—as a loving husband for Ruth. In all these things, God was working behind the scenes to bring about His plan and purpose.
- When our lives feel like they are falling apart, we need to trust that our God has the best in store. He so often provides friends who are more than willing to help. We aren't meant to do life alone.

If you're in that place today, God may have already provided someone in your life. I want to encourage you to be willing to trust, to be willing to let others help. Allow God to show you who He's placed in your life. Remember that He is working all things together in a way far better than we could ever ask or imagine.

Read and reflect on Philippians 1:6.

Day 2: Mary Magdalene, Joanna, and Susanna

Let's begin our time together by considering three women, Mary Magdalene, Joanna, and Susanna, who are all mentioned together in Luke's gospel.

Read Luke 8:1–3.

Who is Mary Magdalene? _____

_____

Who is Joanna? _____

_____

Who is Susanna? _____

_____

How were these three women different?

_____

_____

_____

How were they similar?

_____

_____

_____

Notice how Jesus had healed each of them. Remember that earlier in this study, I asked you to consider the commonalities between you and the people in your small group. If you're doing this study alone, it might be helpful to think of the commonalities you have with friends in your life. Either way, you have this in common with friends who are believers. Jesus healed all of you.

Mary Magdalene, Joanna, and Susanna all gave their lives to follow their healer.

How have you given up the comforts of your life to follow Jesus, your healer?

_____

_____

_____

I have to laugh because we know where three or more women are gathered, there tends to be drama. The trap of comparing ourselves to each other had to be real as these women followed Jesus. How do I know this? Women didn't just start being women now! Social media and television have likely increased the issue, but the comparison game is not new.

Ecclesiastes 1:9 reminds us that nothing is new under the sun. Take comfort in the fact our problems aren't new. Now, let's look at what united these women.

What brought them together?
- They followed Jesus at all costs.
- They were personally invested because of what Jesus had done for them.
- They were externally committed by "giving of their own means" to Jesus's ministry.

Where do we read of Mary Magdalene and Joanna again in the book of Luke?

Read Luke 24:1–10.

These women were some of the first to see the empty tomb when Jesus had been resurrected from the dead. They were so committed to Jesus that they were going to take care of His deceased body at the tomb. Now this is a **_deep_** friendship.

I have to wonder what the conversation was like with them on the way to the tomb that day.

>   _Were they worried things were out of control?_
>   _Did they question if Jesus was who He said He was?_

Since they were women, they likely had a Plan A, Plan B, Plan C, and Plan D. I wonder if any of these plans included that Jesus might not be in the tomb?

It would have been easy for Luke not to note that women were the first at the tomb. It subtly reminds us that our role as women within kingdom work is vital. Our work will likely look different than that of the men in our lives. It is imperative that we do what God has called us to do.

What do you feel God has called you to that only you can do?

_____

_____

_____

How can your friend group support you in this effort?

_____

_____

_____

Mary Magdalene, Joanna, and Susanna all gave from their own means toward the ministry of Jesus. What are you personally giving from your own work to further the kingdom?

_____

_____

_____

It is MUCH easier to find your community while walking in your calling.

Don't miss how easy it would've been for this group of three women to be focused on themselves. Surely it would have been easy for them to have been trapped in the comparison game. They had all been healed by Jesus and traveled with Him. Yet instead, we find three women who were so devoted to Jesus that they never lost their focus on following him.

The work Jesus had done in their lives was so great that they never got over it. Their relationships with each other only existed because Jesus had healed them. Although they may not have been friends prior, they now traveled everywhere together.

What would our relationships be like if they were focused on what Jesus had done in our lives? Do you think we'd be less focused on comparing ourselves to our neighbors and more focused on knowing Jesus?

Let's reflect on this today. How can we take the example of these three women and grow in our own lives?

Day 3: Mary and Elizabeth

One friendship that comes to mind when reflecting on women in the Bible is often Mary and Elizabeth. Now, before you read ahead . . .

What do you already know of Mary and Elizabeth?

_____

_____

_____

Now read Luke 1:1–56.

Luke opens his gospel with Elizabeth and Mary. This provides key background information about the lives of John the Baptist and Jesus. John eventually baptizes Jesus, which marks the start of Jesus's earthly ministry.

The social pressure and expectation for explanation of both Elizabeth and Mary's pregnancies had to be intense. Elizabeth was old. We don't know her age, but she was "advanced in years" (Luke 1:7). This is a women's Bible study, so I will state the obvious. It was probably after menopause.

Did Zechariah really want to explain to the angel that his wife had been through menopause? Again, we don't know for certain, but we know it was a miracle for Elizabeth to be with child.

On the other end of the spectrum, Mary was young. She was engaged to be married to Joseph when the angel told her she would be Jesus's earthly mother.

Now, let's pause here. If you are close to beginning your child-bearing years, in the middle, struggling with infertility, or even if you have adult children, you can likely relate to how it must have felt for Mary or Elizabeth.

> *It would have been easy for Mary to be mad.*
> *It would have been easy for Elizabeth to be bitter.*

How many times do we get upset with God for messing up our plans? Mary's plan was to get married to Joseph, yet her faith was strong. Her response was, "May your word to me be fulfilled" (Luke 1:38).

How many times have we been bitter because God didn't give us something in our desired timeline? Specific to this passage, have you been bitter or known someone who was bitter toward God because they weren't able to have children? *Bitterness takes less effort than contentment.*

Luke 1:36 indicates that Elizabeth and Mary were relatives. I wish we knew more about their relationship and what it was like! We know, though, that when Mary found out she was with child, she went immediately to visit Elizabeth (1:39–40), who was around six months pregnant at the time (1:26).

Fast forward to Luke 1:56, where it says Mary stayed with Elizabeth for three months. We can do some elementary math to know 6 + 3 = 9. Mary stayed until it was time for Elizabeth to give birth.

I imagine this time was precious for Mary and Elizabeth. They were both going through a similar situation where it could be easy for social pressure to set in and discourage them. Yet, they spent time together and worshiped the Lord. Remember that Zechariah couldn't speak until after John's birth (1:22, 63–64).

Being human, I'm sure Elizabeth needed Mary's encouragement even as her husband couldn't encourage her with his words. God granted Elizabeth the gift of John leaping in his mother's womb at Mary's arrival. This was a sweet reminder of their holy calling.

Have you had a time in your life when God gave you a holy reminder that you're doing what He's called you to do?

The word that comes to my mind to describe Mary and Elizabeth's friendship is "precious." It was one of those relationships that endured across miles and lasted for a lifetime.

What friendships comes to mind that are precious to you, that have stood the test through hardship and obedience to God?

Today, let's be grateful for the examples of Mary and Elizabeth. Let's pray for God to continue to bless us with women like them in our inner circles of community!

Day 4: Lydia and Priscilla

One of my hopes for this Bible study is that it will ignite a passion for you to continue studying the early church. You might recognize the two names mentioned in the title for today. Today is not about their friendship with each other, though it is likely that they would have known each other, especially since they were connected with Paul. Rather, it is about them personally and their relationships with others.

I want us to take a closer look at each of them. They have much to teach us about creating community.

Read Acts 16:11–15.

What does Scripture tell us about Lydia in this passage?

_____

_____

We know Lydia was living in Philippi when she encountered Paul for the first time. Philippi lacked a synagogue. This meant Paul and the people traveling with him needed to find a place to pray. They went to the river outside the city where they met Lydia.

The mention of her name is significant. Paul goes on to tell her about the jailer and the slave girl he met at Philippi. Luke also took time to explain Lydia's wealth and hospitality. She was a dealer of purple textiles. The mention of her hometown of Thyatira is notable due to the wealth of that city.

What does Lydia's story in Acts teach us about community?

_____

_____

Without hesitation, Lydia invited Paul and his companions into her home. Let's review what had gone on that day. She didn't leave home in the morning anticipating that she would later return with guests. She didn't know that she would encounter Paul, believe in Jesus, and get baptized.

Many of us today have a distorted view of hospitality. *Lydia's story is one of hospitality not of perfection.* Yes, she had the means and I'm sure she had a lovely home. Yet hospitality has little to do with the size or niceness of your home. Rather, it has everything to do with the posture of your heart.

What stresses you most about opening your home to others?

The takeaway from this story? Lydia demonstrates hospitality without hesitation. Don't let your thoughts spiral: Is my home good enough? Are my dishes nice enough? What will we talk about? ***God is simply calling you to be hospitable with what He has given you.*** It might be a one-bedroom apartment, or it might be a large mansion. It doesn't really matter.

Now, let's look at what Priscilla has to teach us.

Read Acts 18:1–3, 18–26; Romans 16:3; and 2 Timothy 4:19.

What do these verses tell us about Priscilla?

Based on these verses, we know she is married to Aquila. They are always mentioned together. We know they were tent makers, and that Paul shared this trade, too. Aquila and Priscilla were close co-laborers with Paul. They made Paul's ministry easier for him as he traveled and shared the gospel. We could go into much more depth, but for the purpose of this study, we will focus on their support.

Women in the church have the ability to make things easier or harder for those serving in ministry. Scripture is clear that Priscilla enabled Paul to reach more people through her support.

How are you helping your church reach more people through your support?

Priscilla's community was anchored in the local church just as we saw with Lydia. Neither of them was "stirring the pot." They weren't looking for the latest gossip. Priscilla didn't use her connection with Paul to gain notability. She humbly served with her husband. Paul took some of his last words recorded in Scripture to tell Timothy to greet them. Can you think of people in ministry who would use some of their final words to speak to you because of the impact you had on them?

Day 5: Self-Reflection

This week we've covered much ground as we've examined several friendships between women in Scripture. We will continue on our journey to biblical community next week as we consider the end of Paul's journey. For now, let's reflect on all God has taught us this week through these women.

Have you spent more time comparing yourself to others around you or focusing on Jesus?

What external pressures have you had on your life this week?

What have you done to avoid being controlled by these external pressures?

Who in your circle do you trust in a similar way to how Mary and Elizabeth trusted each other? If you don't have anyone, what steps can you take to build a relationship like that?

How can you open your home and take steps to build friendships with others?

_____

_____

_____

_____

Some possible ideas: Is there a new family at your church or in your community that might desire new friends? Is there a church staff member and their spouse that might need some extra encouragement?

As we close, here are your reflection questions to finish the week and prepare for your group time together. This is your reminder we will cover these each week as we walk this journey together toward building your biblical community.

What did God reveal about Himself to you in Scripture this week?

_____

_____

How did your understanding of a particular Bible passage deepen this week?

_____

_____

Are there areas of your life where you have struggled to trust God this week? What can you do to better surrender these areas to Him for next week?

_____

_____

How did you reflect God's Word toward others this week? Is there anything you need to confess to God or someone else?

_____

_____

Journal Your Journey

Prayer Requests

Week Four

4

Paul

Our journey together is half-way over. Congratulations on making it to week four! Our prayer is that you're making strides toward fostering a deeper community. We ended last week by focusing on Priscilla and Aquila. They were a part of Paul's inner community during his ministry.

Paul didn't run from the hardships in life. In his epistles, we read about how he spent much of his ministry helping others, even in trying times. The letters of Paul are the parts of Scripture that I reference most often in my personal life.

I mentioned earlier that throughout my career I have been privileged to walk alongside others in helping to solve their problems. Sadly, I have worked with many who have had a strong start to their calling, yet a weak finish. In contrast, Paul is a great example of someone who finished his calling well.

I'd love to say that I have had all my relationships move in this direction. Yet it has not often been so simple.

Working with people is often challenging. Ministry is hard. So is social work. One professional friendship comes to mind from years ago. I had severed ties with an organization and left abruptly after a passionate disagreement. I certainly did not expect reconciliation! Yet that is just what happened. Many years later, the Lord restored that professional friendship for His glory in His timing. As the years have past, I can see now that God used that entire uncomfortable situation for my growth and His glory.

Friendships have seasons.

This week we are examining the final words of Paul to Timothy. We get to see how he concludes his service to Christ. And we get to read about those who were nearest and dearest to him. We read of those who meant so much to Paul that he took the time to share their names and stories. I know we will find commonalities, even as women, to these relationships.

Read 2 Timothy 4:1–22.

What are some observations you can make about this passage?

_____

_____

_____

_____

_____

Do you recall what we studied in 2 Timothy 3:16? Do you think it is coincidence that Paul made such an effort to remind Timothy of the importance of the inspiration of Scripture prior to his final words?

Certainly not! It was very intentional. We read of Paul's final charge to Timothy in chapter 3, before he concludes with his last written words prior to his death in chapter 4.

Write down and be prepared to discuss with your group a relationship you've had that ended naturally, in a good and appropriate way.

Discuss one relationship that ended in a poor way.

Application:

You probably knew this was coming as we consider the topic of community and relationships. Is there a relationship in your life that needs to be restored? I'm not going to tell you it needs to be fully restored now. I'm not God. I will tell you that you should pray toward closure. What is closure? It is simply an end. It isn't open-ended. You may forgive and move on—or it might require some type of work on your end. I want to challenge you to think about this during our time studying Paul's relationships.

Group Time Notes

Day 1: Loss

Let's begin our study today by reading 2 Timothy 4:9–22.

We will reflect back on this passage several times this week. As I mentioned earlier, we know this letter was the last thing Paul ever wrote. He was in Rome. He knew he was about to die.

Paul was not sure of his execution date at the time of writing, but it was close. He wrote to a younger person in the faith, his dear friend Timothy. Paul gets personal in this letter.

Let's pause for a moment. Are you pouring into anyone who is younger than you in the faith? If you don't know, how could you start to identify someone?

Don't miss the fact that Timothy had Paul in his life. And Paul had Timothy. The significance of their friendship is profound. Timothy was the last person Paul wrote a letter to prior to his death.

Who is passing on wisdom to you as Paul did here in this letter? Who is ahead of you in your faith walk?

What can you do to identify people like Timothy and Paul in your life?

Have you heard the phrase, "Talk is cheap"? It is. Experiences are the most valuable possessions we have in this life. *Nothing replaces experience.* And Paul had a lot of it.

Experience fosters wisdom and growth.

Experiences are best with other people. Loneliness tells us we don't need to experience anything. It says we need to be at home, alone. But notice that Paul doesn't tell us all the great things he did alone in his final words. No, he tells us about loss and influential friendships in his life.

I'm thankful Paul didn't sugarcoat things for us in his writings. He starts with loss. Initially, I questioned this and asked, why? But remember, experience fosters wisdom and growth. The losses of friendships in our lives may be what ends up making us wiser.

I'd much rather skip to the good part. Yet there are seasons in our Christian walk that are good hard. They are painful yet growing and purifying. Paul is pleading with us here not to skip the good hard stuff. What are the lessons we've learned in our losses?

Spend some time as you go through your day reflecting on lost relationships. We will continue tomorrow and see what Paul tells us he learned from his losses.

Day 2: Loss and Gratitude

Let's get specific! Re-read 2 Timothy 4:9–18.

Paul addresses two types of people in his closing remarks. The first group of people he mentions are those who have hurt him. The second group of people are those who helped him. ***At times in my own life, I need to remember the bad to be grateful for the good.***

Who was the first person you read in the passage that hurt Paul? What does Paul say about him?

_____

_____

_____

_____

Demas was the first person mentioned by Paul that caused him pain. Paul said Demas deserted him. He abandoned Paul and went to Thessalonica.

Read Philemon 1:24 and Colossians 4:14

What do these passages reveal about Demas and his relationship to Paul?

_____

_____

_____

_____

They had a close relationship. Demas is noted as being a faithful and helpful friend.

Why does Paul tell us he left?
- For the present world.

What does that mean?
- He left for sin.
- He wanted to enjoy the pleasures of the world.
- Paul wasn't worth it.
- Jesus wasn't worth it.

There are people who will come into your life that you will love, yet because of sin they will walk out of your life.

Have you ever stopped to consider how your own sin can affect others in your life?

Sin is sticky. It sticks to everything and everyone it touches. Demas's sin resulted in him leaving and hurting his former friend, Paul. It hurt so deeply that Paul tells us of it here as a charge to Timothy (and us) to be prepared for when people leave us because of sin.

Take a moment to remember a friend or even family member you have lost over sin. How did it feel? How can you protect yourself from letting unconfessed sin hurt others in your life?

Take some time today to reflect on people who have left your life. You might actually be able to reflect with gratitude. If anything, we can cherish what we were taught by those who aren't with us and the memories we had with them.

Day 3: Titus and Alexander

Again, re-read 2 Timothy 4:9–18.

Although it may feel like an oxymoron, how often do you consider that loss can be good?

There are two types of losses in our lives. The first is situational. Demas was a situational loss for Paul. These are losses where a "situation," often unfortunate, occurs and causes loss.

The second type of loss is a maturational loss. I call it a maturity loss. This type of loss involves normal and natural life changes. It might be exciting, that your child got married and you now have an empty nest. Or it could be sad, perhaps the death of a parent. The list can go on. Life is a maturing process. It is full of these types of losses.

What type of maturity losses are on your horizon or are you walking through right now?

_____

_____

_____

Titus is an example of a maturity loss. Paul simply comments that Titus, who was a very faithful preacher of the gospel, is gone.

Sometimes the most hurt we experience in our lives comes from people who leave for the right reasons.

It is important to see that Paul didn't stop Titus. He just reports that he is now alone and wants Timothy to come quickly.

Have you felt alone after a maturity loss in your life? What can you write here about that time to share with your group or a friend this week? I assure you everyone in the room will have gone through similar losses.

_____

_____

_____

Next, we move on to Alexander. Can I be honest? My flesh wants to love 2 Timothy 4:14. Why? Couldn't you write that verse in terms of your own life? It says, "Alexander the metalworker did me a great deal of harm. The Lord will repay him for what he has done."

For example, I could say, "Maple the dog did me a great deal of harm. The Lord will repay her for what she has done." Yes, Maple is my dog, and this is just an example, but you get the point.

What would you say? Who would be your Alexander who has done you a great deal of harm?

_____

_____

_____

Alexander was a coppersmith, in some translations, a metalworker. He was likely a skilled laborer. He evidently had influence, perhaps even wealth. Yet he used his influence to try to harm Paul's ministry. *Have you seen in your own life where faithful people, like Paul, are harmed?*

Let's get more personal. There are people that might be upset with you for creating your own biblical community. They might have influence and it might be hard, but it is worth it.

Is there anyone or any situation that comes to mind as we talk about Alexander?

_____

_____

_____

Day 4: Alone

It isn't fun to be alone when you had planned to be with others. It is even less fun when you thought people were going to show up for you and they didn't.

For many, especially busy moms, quiet and peaceful alone time is cherished. I will be the first to admit that I enjoy the gap of time between when I arrive home and when everyone else comes home. It is a gift of having older children. Sometimes you just need a minute to breathe and think. On the other hand, perhaps you have an empty nest, are single, or are longing to parent. Perhaps you feel so alone and just want company. No matter the situation you find yourself in, we can all relate to Paul's loneliness.

Paul goes on in 2 Timothy 4 to tell us he was alone, and it wasn't by his own choice. He explains in 4:16 that he went before the emperor. Read 2 Timothy 4:16–17.

What does Paul say happened?

_____

_____

_____

Who gave him strength? How so?

_____

_____

_____

Even though all the people in his life were gone, the Lord never left him. Paul continued to press on to what God had called him to do. He boldly testified about Jesus up until the very end.

Here's the great news. **The Lord has never left you.** You may feel as though you've gone before the emperor alone. Your life has been hard, and you've longed to have people beside you. Yet our God has been there all along. He is enough.

Read Psalm 73:26. What is promised to us in this verse?

_____

_____

_____

Aren't you glad Paul didn't give up when things were difficult?

Read 2 Timothy 4:6–7.

What did Paul do in these verses?

_____

_____

_____

_____

Paul knew death was near. Yet he continued to keep the faith. He didn't harbor bitterness.

Bitterness breeds loneliness.

Is there an area of your life where you can sense a seed of bitterness?

_____

_____

_____

_____

Remember our time studying Elizabeth and Mary? Elizabeth could have been bitter about her situation and her inability to have a child earlier in life. Yet God had uniquely prepared her for her calling to give birth to John and minister to Mary.

Don't miss your moment to find community because of bitterness. Ask God to rid your heart of any bitterness today and give you fresh eyes and a renewed desire for relationships in your life.

> *Keep fighting the good fight even when it's lonely.*
> *Finish the race with endurance even when you want to quit.*
> *Keep the faith for the generations who come after you.*

Day 5: Paul's People

We conclude our time with Paul today as we continue with one final study on 2 Timothy 4. Let's see who was with him in his final days. Re-read 2 Timothy 4:9–18.

Who does 2 Timothy 4:11 tell us was with Paul?

Luke is here, again! I don't know that we should have a favorite gospel, but if I did it would be Luke.

Paul is very human for us in 4:11–13. He wants Timothy to get Mark because Mark had been helpful; he had become a dear friend. He mentions that Tychicus had gone to Ephesus. Tychicus is an important person to mention. He is believed to be the person who delivered the letters to the church at Ephesus and Colossae.

As we consider Luke's close friendship with Paul, have you had a friend who stood by your side even in the most difficult times? Would you be willing to share with the group about this friend and their godly character?

_____

_____

_____

_____

I hope as we close this week that you have been awakened to Paul's biblical community. It wasn't without fault, but it was stacked with some major spiritual giants.

Take a minute as we close today to journal your thoughts on how you could help facilitate creating a community like Paul's.

_____

_____

_____

_____

Next week, we press on toward Jesus. I can't wait to see what we can learn from Jesus's earthly relationships.

Here are your reflection questions to finish the week and prepare for your group time together. This is your reminder we will cover these each week as we walk this journey together toward building your biblical community.

What did God reveal about Himself to you in Scripture this week?

How did your understanding of a particular Bible passage deepen this week?

Are there areas of your life where you have struggled to trust God this week? What can you do to better surrender these areas to Him for next week?

How did you reflect God's Word toward others this week? Is there anything you need to confess to God or someone else?

Journal Your Journey

Prayer Requests

Week Five

Jesus

Jesus.

Our faith hinges on the fact that He was who He claimed to be.

It is important for us to remind ourselves often that Jesus became flesh to pay the price for our sin (2 Corinthians 5:21). Paul knew Jesus was worth fighting for to the very end, even when he knew it would cost him his life.

> *It starts with Jesus.*
> *It ends with Jesus.*

Jesus lived on this earth. He was fully God and fully man. Our human brains can't quite wrap our minds around this concept! This week we are going to focus on a specific aspect of Jesus's humanity. Why? For the purposes of our study, Jesus had an amazing community. We already studied Mary Magdalene, Susanna, and Joanna earlier in our time together.

I want you to take time to discuss Jesus's earthly relationships in your group time or with someone else this week. We can learn so much from His time on earth.

Which of Jesus's human friendships surprise you the most? This week we will dive into several facets of Jesus's earthly community.

His community had layers. We read that His followers included women named Mary Magdalene, Joanna, and Susanna, among others. They traveled with Jesus, supported His ministry, and were the ones who announced His resurrection. He then had His twelve disciples and within the twelve He had His three closest friends.

What are the layers of your community? Are you vulnerable with just a few or with the masses? Discuss this in your group or with a friend this week.

_____

_____

_____

_____

I have used the model Jesus laid out for friendship in my own life. God has provided many friends who cheer me on and encourage me in my faith just as these women did for Jesus.

For me, I can keep breaking down my community into smaller layers. Yes, there is a mid-size group that I love spending time with and getting to know. These are the people I interact with the most. Yet they are not the group with whom I am most open and honest about my life.

Why?

Callings often cause confusion.

Your life's calling is not my calling. Jesus's calling was not the same as His disciples.

It can be easy for someone in your circle of friends to get confused over your calling. This might simply be because they don't know enough of your story. I say this from experience. Let me remind you that you're the only one called to the specific thing God has asked you to do.

For example, I move at a quick pace. I know it. I own it. It is how God wired me. I jokingly say that it is both a gift and a curse. My larger circle of friends may think I'm running right off the burnout cliff. My inner circle knows I ran off that cliff over 15 years ago! Yet my inner circle knows I have put intentional safeguards in place that help me slow down. They know the hard questions to ask me.

It is not necessary that I explain my calling and entire life story to all of the friends in my larger circle. You shouldn't feel the need to either. Friendships are not conditional on knowing everything. They are about furthering kingdom work and the gospel message.

This leads us to the concept of the inner circle. I pray you are in the process of identifying those people for you.

Take time in your group or with a friend to consider how you are feeling about establishing your own community. Is it harder than you thought? What is something good that has come from your participation in this study?

_____

_____

_____

_____

_____

I'm going to pause here to remind you that **any friendship worth having takes work.**

Let's take this week to learn from our Savior. Colossians 1:16 says it beautifully, "All things have been created through Him and for Him." Rest here today. He's got this!

Application:

How can you be like Jesus this week in your friendships? What note of encouragement can you write? What can you do to serve a little extra within your church? What is a topic you can discuss with co-workers that could spark conversations about your faith? How can you (within your own community) encourage others?

Group Time Notes

Day 1: Mary, Martha, and Lazarus

Empathy.

It can be a confusing word. Merriam-Webster defines empathy as, "Being aware of and sharing another person's feelings, experiences, and emotions."

Empathy does not equal agreement.

Empathy says I care about how you feel. Empathy is part of what we call our emotional intelligence (E.Q.). We all either have or do not have a high emotional intelligence level. Jesus had the perfect E.Q.

He showed incredible empathy to His friends and followers. One of the best examples of this is demonstrated in Jesus's relationship with Mary, Martha, and Lazarus. Jesus cared for them. They had developed a deep friendship. They welcomed Jesus into their home where Mary poured perfume on His feet while Martha made preparations within her home.

Read John 11:1–44.

What did the Scriptures establish in verse 4?

_____

_____

_____

God is going to do what brings Him the most glory.

I would imagine that Martha and Mary were frantic about trying to get Jesus to Lazarus. Meanwhile, Jesus decides to wait forty-eight additional hours before heading their direction.

Is there a situation in your life right now where you know God will do what brings Him glory, but you really just want Jesus to fix it on your terms?

_____

_____

_____

We read in John 11 about when Jesus spends time with the sisters. It always makes me laugh when I read 11:21. I would totally be Martha. I would have been eagerly waiting at the gate longing to express how Jesus should have come sooner.

Mary then comes to Jesus in a different posture of grief. The context here is important. Deaths and funerals within Jewish culture involved professional mourners. They would weep with the loved ones of the family. They sought to have a community around them in times of loss.

If you read to the end of chapter 11, you know that Jesus raises Lazarus from the dead.

The part I want us to focus on is the shortest verse in the entire Bible. It may be small, but it has huge implications. John 11:35 records two words: "Jesus wept."

Who is the most recent person you've wept with?

You may not have yet experienced this level of friendship. I pray you have. Although Jesus could have come on the scene and immediately raised Lazarus from the dead, He instead chose to show empathy.

He wept.

Jesus didn't weep because all hope was lost. He wept because He cared about the pain His friends felt. He wept first. He raised Lazarus second.

Sometimes we need to sit and cry. Cry first. Fix what you can later. Jesus chose to raise Lazarus. You may not be able to fix the trial for your friend or loved one, but I assure you that empathy is enough.

Does empathy come naturally to you?

Is there a situation you can reflect on where you've either shown empathy or received it?

Day 2: The Twelve

Grocery pick-up was a game changer for me. It saved me so much time! One time during Covid, I went to get my order. I never checked it. I simply opened my trunk, and they loaded it. I went on my way. I got home and started to unload when I quickly realized that something was WAY wrong. Did I order imitation crab meat? Are those chicken livers?

They had accidentally switched my groceries with someone else's stuff! The store manager was kind and gave me my actual groceries, but they couldn't take the others back due to health restrictions. I never realized before that day what you could learn about someone by seeing their groceries. It is a lot! I've pondered what they were going to do with that food for quite some time now.

This got me thinking about my friend's groceries. What do they put in their cart? Do we buy similar things? What would I be surprised that they buy?

Our grocery orders should be different from our friend's. We ought to have different tastes and styles. Would you want to be friends with yourself?
For me, that would be very boring!

I tend to gravitate toward people who are different than me. On a recent personality test, I scored 50% extraverted and 50% introverted. It really depends on the day, I suppose! This is probably why I have friends who are in both categories.

You don't have to overthink the qualities of those you choose to be in community with right now. I have several close friends who are closer to my parents' age than to mine. Age is just a number. Our spiritual age matters more than our chronological age when thinking about our community.

Jesus gathered His group of disciples with specificity.

Matthew 10:2–4 gives us the names of the disciples. List them here:

Aren't they dramatically different from each other? He chose a tax collector, and He chose fishermen! Jesus set such an example for us in community. He selected a very diverse crowd! Yet He used the strengths of each to accomplish His mission.

What did He ask of His disciples?

They were asked to leave everything!

What have you been asked to leave behind as you follow Jesus?

How are you choosing your close friends and community?

Let's go deeper. Tomorrow we will dive into Jesus's closest circle of three men. Reflect today on how you can be more intentional in surrounding yourself with the right people.

Day 3: The Inner Circle

Community is easily romanticized. The reality of an "inner circle" has little to do with fun and more to do with helping carry the load. It might even be a heavy load.

Have you ever wished you didn't know something about someone? I've had several of those situations over the years. It's tough. Sometimes I wish I could just unknow the information.

Perhaps you're familiar with the new feature on the iPhone where you can edit text messages after they're initially sent to another iPhone. This has been a game changer for me. We can now change our minds on what we want to say even after we've sent the message.

Sadly, we don't get to unknow information about someone. This is why the inner circle helps carry the weight of the heaviest things in life.

What is on your heart that is heavy right now?

_____

_____

_____

Peter, James, and John were part of Jesus's inner circle. I wanted to have a profound reason to tell you why Jesus chose three, but I don't have one. The only thing I can say is that Jesus chose them to be the closest to him. This meant they saw and experienced more than the others.

Read Luke 8:49–56.
What does this passage say about the inner circle?

_____

_____

Now, let's look at another instance in Scripture where the three are listed together.

Read Luke 9:28–36.
What does this passage say about the inner circle?

_____

_____

Were the other disciples jealous? We don't know. ***We do know that with more knowledge comes more responsibility.*** This applies to life and community.

Peter, James, and John had a front row seat to the most significant events of Jesus's ministry.

Who has a front row seat in your life? Who are you most honest with?

_____

_____

_____

_____

I could offer all kinds of theologians' opinions on why Jesus chose these three specifically, yet we're really not entirely sure why. Sometimes we have to be okay with not knowing all of the information. It is enough that Jesus brought them along with Him at big events. We don't need any more information than that.

> *Yes, they were leaders.*
> *Yes, they were faithful.*
> *Yes, they were instrumental in forming the church.*

This should free you. You don't have to have a grand reason for why people end up in your inner circle. I know mine was accidental to me, yet extremely intentional from the Lord. Allow God to help you form your innermost and most vulnerable friendships. Be honest. Invite them into your life as Jesus did with these three disciples.

Don't miss the fact that Peter, James, and John were there to help bear the weight of the ministry Jesus carried on His shoulders. God was using this time to prepare them for what was ahead. At times it can look glamorous to be in a certain person's inner circle. I assure you, though, that the inner circle in biblical community was not merely there for fun. The people you've chosen should push you toward what God is calling you to do and help carry the weight of this world.

Reflect today on those closest to you. Who is at the other end of your 2 AM phone call if something goes wrong? I have to laugh because my friends put their phones on "Do Not Disturb," but you get the point!

_____

_____

_____

Day 4: Public Perception

Wouldn't it be nice if we didn't have to care about our reputation? Or if we didn't care what people thought of us? I'm not a self-identified people pleaser, but I am mindful of my reputation. The majority of the time I don't care how others perceive me nor do I try to please them.

In full transparency, though, writing this study has been a time where I cared more about what the readers (you) think. This comes from a place of cheering for you to have amazing friendships. I feel the healthy weight of guiding you on this journey through Scripture to that place.

You have a reputation that involves how you are perceived by others. Now, please don't misunderstand me. Don't become a people pleaser because I told you to consider your reputation! I do want to encourage you, though, to narrow down what you're known for in your community.

Consider this: What do people think of when you come to mind? Write down a word or two?

No, today is not about a friendship in Jesus's life. It is about the public perception of Him by others. It is about His reputation.

Read Luke 5:15.

What does it say about the peoples' reaction to Jesus?

Jesus came to earth with the end in mind. Every relationship and interaction He had in His earthly ministry pointed toward that goal. Jesus knew He had to choose those who were closest to Him.

You should desire to be known for your faith.

You should be known as someone who is like Jesus.

You shouldn't desire to be known for your clothing or weight.

Are you known for your faith? How so?

_____

_____

_____

_____

Are the people in your inner circle pushing you toward your end goal? Explain your thoughts here.

_____

_____

_____

The people in your community should encourage you to do what God is calling you to do. Focus on this today.

Day 5: Peter

Peter denied Jesus three times. I remind you of this because even though he messed up, Jesus still was close to him. In fact, Peter was the one who preached the bold sermon in Acts 2.

You may have a Judas or a Peter in your life. Judas left Jesus's life. Judas betrayed Jesus the night before He died. He didn't get to be a part of any additional ministry. Peter denied Jesus three times yet repented and served faithfully for the rest of his life.

I encourage you to cherish the "Peters" in your life. It is hard. Even though they may have hurt you in the past, they are godly friends. Jesus gave so much grace to Peter. We can show that same grace.

The question to consider as you think of the "Peters" in your life is this: "Are you all moving in the same direction toward Jesus?"

Read Hebrews 12:1.

What does this tell us about our spiritual journey, our "race"?

_____

_____

_____

_____

Notice, it doesn't just say, "Get rid of." No, it is stronger than that. It says, "Throw off anything that hinders." You may have people that you need to throw off kindly from your path. In fact, following Jesus is going to cause some people to weed themselves out of your circle. We need to be alright with this.

Remember, Jesus remains ever so gracious. He was kind to people while on earth. He is kind to us now as He is seated in heaven. There is never an excuse for us to be unkind to someone in our lives, even if they have hurt us.
As we close the week, here are your reflection questions to finish the week and prepare for your group time together. This is your reminder we will cover these each week as we walk this journey together toward building your biblical community.

What did God reveal about Himself to you in Scripture this week?

How did your understanding of a particular Bible passage deepen this week?

Are there areas of your life where you have struggled to trust God this week? What can you do to better surrender these areas to Him for next week?

How did you reflect God's Word toward others this week? Is there anything you need to confess to God or someone else?

Journal Your Journey

Prayer Requests

Week Six

6

Stronger Community

I'm so excited we are at week six of our time together! We've taken a beautiful journey through Scripture. My prayer is that you are well on your way to building a stronger community.

Our time would be incomplete without addressing the hardships of growing in deep biblical community. What did we say at the beginning? **Meaningful friendships take hard work.** The words "grace" and "gratitude" come to mind over and over again as we walk this journey of sanctification.

I can't put into words how thankful I am for my friends. Yet still, I want to be clear that we are far from perfect. The majority of our friend group is very direct. You can imagine our conversations at times!

As a group, we've celebrated many wins together. To be honest, though, there have probably been more hardships than wins. The reality is that we're all going to face hardships. During the difficult days it is much better to have others standing by your side, believing in you, and supporting you. That is the hope of biblical community. And that is my hope for each of you!

When hardship comes, people are going to see the real you. You don't want it to be the version they've never seen before. You want to be known already.

Paradoxically, the trade off with being known by a biblical community is just that: You are known. You must be open and transparent with your community, honest and candid. The result? **You are seen, heard, and deeply loved.**

What a joy it is to rejoice that we are completely known by God. He knows every detail about our lives, yet He has showed His grace by giving His Son, Jesus, to cover the cost of our sin.

My hope is that each day of this week's study is practical and applicable to your life. Remember that each of these biblical lessons we've covered cannot be done without grace, trust, and time.

I'd like to encourage you to consider the questions below and be prepared to discuss them with your group.

Does showing grace come easy to you or is it hard?

_____

_____

_____

_____

Do you overthink or regret what you have said to others?

_____

_____

_____

_____

Do you struggle with gossip? Do you say more than what needs to be shared?

_____

_____

_____

_____

What makes someone trustworthy? How do we work on becoming more trustworthy?

_____

_____

_____

_____

Application:

Consider ways you can hold yourself accountable to be a good friend after this study is complete. If you want authentic and honest friendships, how can you grow to be a more trustworthy friend yourself? How can you prepare yourself now for the hardships you will face in the future? How can you help others in the hardships they are currently facing?

Group Time Notes

Day 1: In Hiding

Have you ever hidden from someone who came by your home unannounced?

I hope I'm not the only one that has a history of this. A close friend popped by unannounced one afternoon at the beginning of our friendship. The front of our home had many windows and I saw the car pull up. It was December. I probably don't have to say anything else except the word, "December," for you to understand the insanity of our schedule. I don't think I had washed my hair in days. My house was a disaster. I was SURE if she came into my mess, our friendship would be over.

I did what any logical person would do at that moment. I fell on the floor by the couch. I hid from her and told my children to be quiet. I just could not grasp letting her into my real life.

I reflect back on this story and laugh. You can be assured she has now seen my house at its worst. I'm sure I've seen hers in the same condition. Yet at the time, I believed the lie that I needed things to be perfect in order to have friends. I wanted to go to lunch, but I needed her to think I had it all together.

Have you ever had a season of friendship where you felt like you had to have it all together?

We don't have time in life to be friends with people who won't love us for who we are. Women have to show grace toward each other in the midst of our busy lives.

What does Romans 12:9 tell us about love?

I was hypocritical with my new friend. I didn't want her to really know that there are times when my life is crazy.

I'm sure that there will be women who make it this far in this Bible study and still say they have to have everything perfect to invite people over or have their life all together to make friends. Why? If I'm waiting to be perfect to invite people over, it won't ever happen.

Remember, you *can't* do it alone.

You need to work to get over what is holding you back.

I asked you the first week of this study what you were worried that people might find out about you. Look back. Are you still concerned about it, or have you refocused in our weeks together?

Let's reflect on removing anything in our lives that keeps us from the community God wants us to have.

Day 2: Our Words

I have realized that the biggest hindrance for adult women in friendships is often the tongue. A wise friend shared with me early in my marriage that the hardest part of being an adult was choosing when not to say something. At the time, I thought this was silly. I didn't think I struggled in that area. I could not have been more wrong. I've reflected on those words almost every day since that conversation fifteen years ago.

Our words have the power to speak life or tear others down.

How have you used your words today? Have you spoken life into someone or torn them down?

_____

_____

_____

_____

Our actions are reflective of our attitude.

What does this mean? The action of speaking words comes from our attitude. Luke 6:45 tells us that out of the overflow of our heart the mouth speaks.

There are numerous individuals recorded throughout Scripture who used their words wisely. Jesus, of course, is the ultimate example of using words wisely. He knew His words carried weight and He used them carefully around others.

Read Philippians 2:1–30.

What is your favorite part of this passage?

_____

_____

_____

_____

I often return to Philippians 2. It brings me back to the center of the gospel. In it, Paul was writing to the church at Philippi. This church was in trouble. Euodia and Syntyche were two notable women in the church. They were causing dissension (Philippians 4:2).

What? Two women were upset with each other and caused trouble? Theologians agree that they were probably building "teams" or getting people to agree with them.

Paul opens Philippians 4 with the connection, "Therefore . . ." Here, he signals that he is serious. I'd even say he is begging the Philippians to be like-minded.

Now you may think Paul's concern is not necessary, but my friends, women can cause chaos and disunity in the church with their words. Men can do the same thing. I'm writing to you, women, and I want to caution us to not be like Euodia and Syntyche.

The best antidote for wanting to say negative things is gratitude. Let's say you're in a negative conversation and you feel pressure to be negative. You may know the situation is grim. Yet you can always say, "I'm so thankful for _____." You have the power to provide the positive spin in a negative conversation.

I assure you that people are attracted to positive people. We crave good in a negative world.

I want to challenge us today. What if we spent a whole day without speaking a negative word? I know, I'm asking a lot of some of us! I'm right there with you. Yet, Colossians 4:6 is clear. Our conversations should be positive. Let's focus on this today.

Day 3: Our Time

The older we get, the more we understand that there are seasons of life. Time doesn't get slower, and we can't add any more hours to the day. I won't say never, but I'm probably not the person who should teach time management skills. I have learned time management strategies out of desperation, but I am no expert on this subject.

I do know this, though: *Face-to-face time is the only way to build community.*

Our journey to parenting was unique in the adoption of our daughter. We ended up on the other side of the world. For twenty-nine days we were in Africa with people we did not know, or least did not know well. The one thing we had, though, was time. We had more time than ever before. I remember the most exciting event one day was when the coke truck made a delivery to our hostel!

I have since craved going back to those days and I've lamented the fact that I can't spend that amount of time with my other friends. Why? Time spent face-to-face is the only way to build a meaningful community. You can make long distance friendships work, but nothing is sweeter than time across the table from each other.

Now, if you knew the reality of how hard those days were, you'd think I was crazy. There are many parts of that trip I hope never to experience again, but as I look back, I enjoyed every single conversation. God allowed so much loss to happen during those days, yet He knew we would be sustained through community.

It would have been very tempting for me to lock myself in my room and isolate myself. More days than not, it would have been easier to get back into bed and pull up the covers. I'm not an awesome person because I chose to get out of bed those days. But I got up because I knew the people downstairs needed me and I needed them.

After that trip, I now prioritize my time differently. I wanted more friends like the ones I'd grown so close to in that hostel.

Ask yourself these questions . . .
- When was the last time you lingered at the table after dinner?
- When was the last time you had an uninterrupted coffee meeting with someone?
- Do you proactively plan time to grow friendships?
- How many hours did you spend on your phone last week?
- Could you adjust your calendar to make time in your schedule?

I'm not asking these questions to make you feel guilty. I'm asking these questions because many times we don't even realize how we spend our time.

To build authentic community, we need to make time.

All of the biblical relationships we examined over the last five weeks took time to build. Which one sticks out to you from our study? Why?

_____

_____

_____

_____

Read John 10:10.

What are the three things Satan attempts to do?

_____

_____

_____

_____

Ladies, Satan is stealing our time. He's convinced us through numbing activities that we are at maximum capacity.

As we end today, let's focus on the freedom we have to create space for relationships. What can you take off your calendar to make time for building community?

_____

_____

_____

_____

Day 4: Trust

The core of any relationship is trust. I quoted Henry Cloud earlier in this study as saying, "Trust is the fuel for all of life."

What do we do when we don't trust?

I'm sure many of us struggle trusting people. However, we'll never be able to build the communities we want—authentic and transparent communities—without first being vulnerable.

Jesus didn't stop trusting the other disciples because Judas betrayed him.
Paul didn't stop trusting others because Demas left him.
Mary Magdalene didn't lose trust in Jesus amidst the world going dark.
Elizabeth did not lose trust in God when she wasn't able to bear children.

The list could go on and on from the individuals we've studied together.

Our hope must be anchored in our belief and trust in God.

What does Hebrews 6:19 tell us?

How do we respond when someone we have grown to trust fails us?

Read the following and write down what we should do:

Ephesians 4:15

Galatians 6:1–2

Trust comes with time.

For those who have failed us, perhaps we could try trusting them with little things. We could create opportunities to give real feedback to each other. It might feel weird at first and it might be uncomfortable, but it could create opportunities for growth.

To be clear, though, you do not have to be in close community with those you cannot trust.

There are some people in my life who I don't trust. I am kind to them. I have a general friendship with them. Yet I don't share a lot about my life. It is okay to distance yourself from someone who has betrayed your trust. The Holy Spirit will guide you.

Reflect today on who you struggle to trust and why.

_____

_____

_____

_____

Day 5: Final Challenge

Here's my charge to you on our final day together:

- You are worthy of having a community around you.
- Your life is not so messy that you can't let people into it.
- God designed you for community with Him and other believers.
- Building biblical community is worth energy and hard work.
- There isn't a shortcut to meaningful friendships.
- Face-to-face time together is the only way to build lasting friendships.
- The Holy Spirit is our Helper when trying to do difficult things.
- Scripture has given us all we need for our time on earth. We have to choose to study it.

Let's reflect on our growth in our six weeks together:

What are new things you are taking from our time together into your sanctification journey?

_____

_____

_____

I asked you early on what you were most afraid of your group/friends finding out about. Is this still something you are concerned about or did it change over the last six weeks?

_____

_____

_____

Who is someone you feel like God is leading you to let into your life as a friend?

_____

_____

_____

How have you fallen more in love with Jesus over the course of the study?

_____

_____

_____

Lastly, how is your biblical community? Has it grown in our time together?

_____

_____

_____

What is the next step you feel God is calling you to after our time studying scripture?

_____

_____

_____

You are loved by your Savior and prayed for by our team as you close this book.

We are praying Numbers 6:24-26 over you. "May the Lord bless you and keep you; The Lord make his face shine upon you and be gracious to you; the Lord turn his face toward you and give you peace."

Journal Your Journey

Prayer Requests

Notes

Notes

Notes

Notes

Notes

Notes

WOMEN OF JOY™

Are you ready for the best weekend ever?

When is the last time you had a weekend away to focus on your relationship with friends and, most importantly, God?

Women of Joy is a three day, two-night weekend where thousands of women gather in the name of Jesus to worship the Lord, study God's Word, and fellowship with friends.

It is the original Women's Weekend Getaway. It is truly the best weekend ever!

Meet our speakers and artists, and find the Women of Joy event nearest you at **womenofjoy.org.**